VOYAHER

Published by **crater era**

View and join our inclusive art house online at craterera.com

Connect with us on social media @craterera

Business and other inquiries can be directed to our email support at support@craterera.com

VOYAHER

A FOUR ACT COLLECTION OF SHORT POEMS

Elijah R. Abramson, M.D.

CRATER ERA || SAN FRANCISCO || 2025

PUBLISHED BY CRATER ERA

Copyright © 2025 by Elijah Abramson

All rights reserved. Published in the United States by crater era LLC, San Francisco, CA.

No part of this publication may be reproduced or transmitted in any form or by any means without the express written permission of the publishing company.

For information regarding permissions, please write to crater era at support@craterera.com. The company is based in northern California, specifically the San Francisco Bay Area.

https://www.craterera.com

ISBN: 9798284843130

First American edition, May 2025

In loving memory of

Isaiah Kyle Abramson

January 1995 -- September 2024

PREFACE

I think a revival of poetry at the present era is of the utmost importance. The brief, flexible, beautiful short-story telling that led to some masterful classics has gone by the wayside. Multimedia and social media have drawn attention away from the art and beauty of the written word.

Thankfully, the art is not fully lost. Art in theater as well as music is very much poetic, just in different form. Nonetheless, I think a return to the written word and short-story telling of poetry would be ideal. In writing this collection, I intended for it to be digested and marketed and thought of as Tik Toks or Instagram stories, but in writing format not audio and video format. Some of it may resonate with you. Some of it may not. Some of it you may not like, some of it you may love. Some of it you may find humorous or tragic or offensive. However you feel about it is ok.

I chose poetry because I think in writing in this format, as others before me have, highlights the art in imperfection because perhaps what you perceive to be a mistake was actually intentional. Perhaps it was a mistake. But either way, it may slow you down and minimize the doomscrolling that social media can perpetuate. Take the time to read, read slowly. Read the whole thing in one sitting or read one poem a week. Do what feels right to you. Most importantly, poetry forces you to use your imagination. The words are just words but to create the feel and the setting requires you to put the time and energy into doing it for yourself. I think that has value.

Hopefully you find it enjoyable to read through. Some of the writing is tragic, some of it is comedic. My only recommendation is this: if you are easily offended, do not read this collection. This is not non-fiction in nature. It is not meant to be taken literally. Take a breath, take a break from doomscrolling, take a break from the anxiousness embedded in excessive political correctness. Read them out loud to friends, silently to yourself, or out loud to yourself. Enjoy.

1
In the beginning

Anorexia

18 years old
crossed the country
left her family
but somehow did not yet
know yourself
herself
and ended up
flying united
every weekend
because
she did not eat
could not eat
knew the heimleich
but did not realize
she was crazier than her roommate
BMI 18

The major

She said she was premed
because she needed to heal herself
but instead imposed
a fact
It
showed us
that her
Factitious
disorder
was
Impotent
or
imposed
on herself

The major 2

So then what had happened
fue
the fuego was lit
the green light
red cardinal
became a source of blackness
darkness
and now listen carefully
this is dr. e talking
and the one truth is
words matter and actions speak louder than words.
So
Have ing saying
That.
When I Speak of Blackness and Darkness
This is Not the Race.
This is the Soul.
Because White Souls and Black Souls
Do Not Equate to Complexion.
Colorism is Racism.

The Major Three

She is irish and scottish.
Christian.
A quote un
Quote believer.
But religion perpetrates more bullshit than good shit.
Especially Christianity.
Ffs
U n I no
IT IS THE TRUTH!
So "she said"
She was going to be a doctor.
But that was yet another lie
She told herself because
She would always become
some1
Who did not hear a who
Did not trust a soul
With her white skin.
Blonde hair.
Black Soul.
UOENO
But she would have four who new.
Two kings. Two queens.
She failed out. Could not make it.
She never became a doctor.

The motor Psych culman

So she met a man
Who at heart was still a lost soul
Lost boy.
Long story.
Narcissist as she said
Butttttt
And not a big juicy butt.
Just a tiny one.
So they became fast food friends
Junkies without the drugs.
Except weed. He smoked a shit ton of weed.
And he was hooked on her.
Two youngest children.
Lost.
Together.
And Thir STiry
Was Just Beginning.

Bi Polar Ex Press

Diagnostic
Statistically
Manually
Transmission.
Now colloquium Lee.
What happens is this.
People are up
Den
Dey
Go
Abajo
En
Frente
Friend ey?
But unless
They spend crazy
Delusional on self
or others
Entonces
question pasas
Passes
And
The ups and downs are not
BPD
But

B
Personality
Deeeez
Nuts
Order.
Borderlinepersonalitydisorder!
That is her diagnosis.
The second I have given.

Graduation

She was lost.
Communicating biology.
Mastered it.
But now it begged to
Bee
Gin.
Gin and juice!
Not yet…. thats downs
Tariffs.
There was a fork
In the Road and
She went Off Roading.
Went back in 2 her shell
And Liz brought Nicholas
and his stash of his stache
To stack a stack of blank
paper
So they went to a bitch
town on the beach.
And wanted two raise
Kids to fulfill a dream
Dat shit was a scam dey
tooled them selfishes.
And so began the next FAZE.
A real like life video game.
Where the worst thing happened.
They were two fish that were self fish
and thot they wuz self dress for loss
or less at ross.

Jack and Jill

Nick and Liz
Sitting
Inna
Money tree
With nom one Y.
Communicating at stanford.
Lost in paly high
along with the Gunn
Going off at that school.
Kids killing kids.
Kids killing themselves.
Because that campus is a shitshow of
lost souls paper chasing paper planes.
So they lives Ames
Port Washington
by the populous
Popular
Dune
Surfer
Pillar
POINT.
beach.

King E.

8 march.
0404.
Flight 1993.
Born day.
San Mateo
Peninsula
The Mill Coffee shop.
Is a story for A
Both a.
Day.
He started swimming on the path
while Liz was biking
these blocks
over with Tyler the
Crater
and a bike that she sure
new
 wasn't a milli like Lil Weezer.
Initials:
Equal
Rights
Amandament.

A star was born.

His grandmother
Nana new.
He is gift Ed tea.
Blue.
Then purple.
White
and Jewish.
But not half of shit.
Full.
Of happiness and life.
But a victim already.
Munchausen syndrome by proxy.
Because Liz munch house syndrome.
So eminem was M&M
and blond e like her.
So hey mama.
Hi mama.
I am here.
I am him.
He is me.
They are them.
You are awwwww FULL.
Pretty hurts.
And so does the truth.

TWO

so when he was two
number two
came in.
Zeke was quiet.
Ed was going to educate him.
Because Liz was a whim
Sick all.
The time.
Zeke was his shadow.
Mini me.
Curly hair though.
So until you see Los Angels.
He looked into the stars
and hit some pars
with his bars
and Ed led because those
who bred would barely even
keep them fed.

TWO TWOS

My story is His Story.
I am Him.
He is me.
Don't be scared because those
are Big Statements.
But humble ones because like Ed said
in bed and at work.
"I'm just a guy."
buttttttttt purrrrrr
HAPPS
nice guys finish first
and the girl can still finish second

Two three trap.

One four six
Six four one
Two for 8
Did not ate
or Eat
But carbs and
she pounded caffeine
Star Bucks.
Not Safe at home
or Safe aWay.
So they
Scrambled not eggs
Scrabble. Cereal was all they
ate.
And tort y yuhs gene liked
So E and Z
Played
Tennis.
Golf.
Baseball.
Basketball.
Skim boarding.
Boogie
Board
ING!

Girl!

Ed said it better be a she.
And he got what he wanted.
A1 sister.
But little sis
Ter Did she Know
She was In 4 It.
She bought a King
Bed
But wants to be a Queen?
Str8 up
or rainbow
You no
Love is Love
BUTTT
(ideally a nice 1 of 1)
as champagne
Mami
dice
Know Yaself!
She doesn't.

Girlllllllllll !

She ran
circle
around mi tierra CE!
By lyk Lee
six moths
Up stairs
down stairs
every stare
was cuz she is blon duh
Too.
Mid dull Chai old.
But thot ian
A is the monroe
Na an A LIAR
50 shades of shit
She is from Ga Ana.
Sorry that was a tangent
Not how a man dittttt
But she wanted 2 bee
the bee that stung
But she was three of
FORE before.
Liz kicked her
Out house
Sorry I mean

Out da
1 four six six six
House.
LVN
248.
868.
7 ate
Sev
EVEN
One!!!

the baby.

she walked
before she
Ran
and she was
adored
especially bi nD
Because
She knew who she was
an extrovert.
popular but no interest
In
Poplar ity.
A free bird.
A sweet sweet girl.
Short in stature
But powerful in soul.
And now you feel
the rush
of a cool breeze
Over her head
pero
perro
Habibi
Me sor ray
Me da se

Pa
Papa mami
Fucked her up too.
She got fucked too.
And not the good Kind.

_____

2
In the middle

the baby walks

so the baby
was carried
by three
Triplets
ski ing
thru
snow
and trust me
ed nor zeke
nor Lexi
nor Lila
ZELL ed
no comp
En
sacion.
They
were victim iiiiiii
zed.
but they stopped
the numb / encore
attempt to protect the babe y.
from liz n nick.
all four
were fore
Toast.
but finally
at 1 age
the girl walked.

the genie us is con firm Ed.

so.
Cuando
El
Ed
Wuz inn
1 ST street
Grade.
All A's.
Already.
Fucking crazy.
SOOOOO
in first grade he sat
by him
Self.
And did 5
Th
Gradewework.

Then after winter
BREAK!
hut hut
he landed in second grade with
a protect Ivan friend.
Who made sure no one fucked wit him.
Cuz the streets are crazy.

Bullies on playgrounds
Carry ing
Generations of
generating
Generational
TRAUMA ALERT!!!!

GRADE 3

So now with The build up
of jeen YUHS
in a boy.
He had no leader.
No pair unto who he could trust.
Who he could learn about life.
The munch house en which he
lived was a place
where
Violence
was ultraviolet
turning VIOLET
violet.

violent.

play action FAKE!

nick washed
not clothes.
mouths with soap.
life with lies.
narcissistic personal ity disssss
track order.
so now he brought
ed to school late
Corn meal for breakfast
Capri
SUN
for lunch
y nada para la cena.
She made cena.
While he beat her @$$.
once.
she cried.
but denied.
no one cried wolf but the
boyed was pissed.
and he was a Kid without indicudi.
For now.

Bully.

Violet was a shade of blue
And his second heart
So when he got socked
At 5 in 5 despite being not five
He punched back once.
HARD.
The principle of the bully
Hurt kids hurt kids prolly
Cuz primo
Que pasa es is
That he stood up and
got sent to the judge
Principal this time.
He was scared not of the bully
but of the authority
Two adult women.
And guess what his sentence
Had?
.
Period.
Japan.
White and red makes pink.
Or blue like the Pacific Ocean?
Cuz the sentence was a period.
There was nothing.

He. Did. Nothing. Wrong.
But He did not yet realize what exactly that mean T.

Battle citizen ship.

Middle
Not child but school began
and he was deathly hallowed
with fear.
The change that he never could tolerate
The beginning of the true reveal
of generating generation all trauma.
Liz blacked out talking
Nick just smoked in the back
Garage
by the laundry garbage machine.
En ton ces when
Taylor
pierced the court
He had no idea how to bounce
the dropped ball in the hoop
at 10 feet.

SPORTS!

Soccer then baseball
Then basketball
then track
Den no wrestling lmfao
solo
Solamente
Sol angel no Los Angeles
so he went from running
4 hunnid to
sub sequencely
pitching a perfect
Juego.
Crazzzzy amirite???
Sub 7
Mile.
And basketball!
Can not rum member
eggs cat ally
But
He was on the 7A or B team
as a center!
And he defended the paint
despite no respite at home
and no history of organized ho
oops before.

Mind you.
He was already the best LLBean
I mean LL beisbol pull ayer.
Then he won
Citizenship award in 8 in 00 or 01 or 02.

Hella locals only.

Him Bee High
Escuela Cabrillo
Unified
At lewis 1.
was when he real isaiah'ed
that social Lee
He had no circle.
1 over zero.
remember then ame was
His song as he walked home
and mowed to the cows
He had 2 much hand
I'ed
coordination to
Fit
Inwit
The Nerdz
cuz captain under pants
was his comic
but at the Sam Ed
Time.
He was top of the sorting hat
Grief in door
but also the one throwing
No Hit Hers

and Prefect Games
at based ball.
And that was not enuf
So Ed did also
polo en la aqua
y basketball.
So who could really react
and respond and re
Late?

Girls, girls, girls.

Crush
Crash
Into He?
Butt the isaact iss U
was this:

How 2 ass k?
Nick was use less.
Dress for less than less.
So Carey was not YT musically
Either
But she seemed to fw him
Butt he did nt no wat 2 do
so he never axed her out
Bc what did that odd mean?
He led lil girls around the playground
pre escuela but
now in mid and high
School?
No alcohol
No drugs
Just sports, school, family, and FUN.
He was so scared and naive that
He could not roam antic Ally
Ryan Ask

A girl
OUT!
at home.

———

Chemical romance.

U c
T he thing izzy
that
Ed loved all education
and particularly particulate
matter.
Berkelium. Beryellium.
Uranium.
Mercury.
Iron.
Sharpened by the bunsen
BURNER a Count.
Until his friend got fucked with
And cuz he had red hair
Like Eds blonde
strawberry
black
Brown hair actually. Curls
Ed and John had curls.

Mr. John in Japan
had been
Burnt but the Hedwig
Teach Her
was awesome.
Frfr she was the best.
And she went to berkeley
back when that dick was free
not in captivity
Interlude.

Chemistry pt. 2

some how
as a 2
guard
well actually a center
he one won 1 for Juan
and
Den
what had happened was
he was tutoring this
girl who was a senior
in química!
Wtf. Ed was
originally in 1 learning 5
now in 10 teaching 13?
but at least now
with Juan and John
He had started to have some friends
because
now he realized the nerds
at least spoke his language
the jocks just did drugs which
i learned is baaaad
MKAY?
No?
well maybe.

good.
so he taught her well
and she trans
lt
Ion
Ed. Into a capable student!

Stats

That prof was cray.
She had no idea wat was going on.
It was honestly weird.
She basically had him run
Nina ing
The show.
And it was AP
All Playerz.
And he crushed it again.
Ez money.
But as a senior bee Leave
It or not.
Butttttt
A sea gull
Sharted and charted
Its way onto Ed's head
before bed.
But you know what
i think she always knew who he was.
2020.
SE asian women always. Always. Always.
Had/have his back.
ALWAYS.

The real graduation.

U see he thought
5 and 8 were it
but they were promo shuns.
he gave the 2speech
cuz lunchbox
gave him a 92 point
4 game so
she would win.
Now.
Donut get me wrong.
She deserved it.
She and he were both equally
special.
So at end of quarter
it did not matter.
But in nyt Opinion
I think lunchbox had
#metoo issues
before metoo was a thing.
And she was a she.
So was he/him/his
a victim of her #metoo?
Hmphty dump
Ty for the lesson.

First home.

King George
In Berkeley, California.
Public institution.
The greatest university in the world.
Bar none.
Boalt bolted to Berkeley law.
He studied everything there.
The academics.
The people.
Himself.
And then
Peekaboo.
Liz and Nick divorced.
Munch
House
En
Was diving deeply
Under ground.
The house Liz built
Was shattering glass.
Just like
the murder suicide
nextdoor.

1234

Every year
Had its own lessons.
And the most valuable lesson of
The firetrap
Runs
Pink
Ferraris.
I house
Sigma Chi.
Alpha.
KA.
Youtube, google, face
Booked.
Was the protection from the
House of Horror.
Because the House Liz Built
Had became haun Ted Talk.
Ed left. Liz began the boxing in.
These walls were beginning 2 talk.
And Ed was not sure how to defend
His siblings
But the ladies soccer team
had legs
so do the runners
and the ladies on 5 spenz

Black
were not
black or white
BUTTTT
she was fine as hell with body.
If you don't no the answer
Then
go to the den
and axe
Roderick and Rickie.

rod y rick

7 ida
was sprowling
with characters
cuz primo
thats how
berklee
makes
muse ick!
every1 is invited to
da fiesta
y alla
que pasa es
tres amigos
hatch Ed a lifelong
friendshup.

rods boyszn

bro those dudes are hilarioussss
1 barely talked
but that dude smelled like str8 @$$
y el otro
mannnnnnnnnnnn
k pasded
wuz that he studied
n then
kinda just dipped
the other dude had mona y
hella smart dude frfr
but awkward af
after
tierra
mi they got hella
food
they would share
a story
and man trust me
those are stories
that roderic K St. ill
can tell 2 diss día

sammy

Gee, I'll have 2 tell
a lotta stories bout her
cuz she came second
eliana y ed came first
but that girl
had a heart of
platinum.
meanT well.
she just wasnt quite his type writer.
dont get me wrong it was a good ass
time. but it wasnt quite the compatability
match. but how do u match
an artist athlete academic jeen-YUHs
?

sam

an tho lougy
base ically
didnt quite keep his head ringing.
he needed craycray n she is hella normal
so normal that that that
wasnt enough.
carl son evolved a good
class which also happened tubi
a fun time to learn
but then grad2ation
happened.
and finally the parents
came!
to graduation.
after coming up once before.
liz and nick
pathetically perfect 2gether.
so he made sum
friends but mostly
got trapped.
not by sam.
but by liz.
and joke was still on him cccuz
he thought it was nick dropping
charcoal down the chimney.

Alex

nearly a hooper
but a good friend
different background
of course
but thats how it always is for him
because he preaches without preaching one thing:
no violence against yourself or others.
all follows health and happiness.
so Al Neer
Hooped and gamed
Ed games too btw lmfao.
COD, mad Den, 2k, FN soon enough
and they gamed and watched
NWA movie butttt
Al thinks he is a G and trust me.
He ain't.
Weeknd privilege. Weekday privilege.
You don't have to be white to have privilege.
You don't have to be black to not have It.
Despite what summay say.

20 15 5

Ed sent out an SOS
when his knee burst into flames
Like the phoenix.
And Nick and Liz did not give a shit.
Nothing new there.
But CP3 went +8000 on a $1 bet
to get a trip dub.
Buh-LEEEEd-THAT!
Ironic right?
He just finished studying about
boomer old people shit that happens
to the Nee Wen you crank it the
wrong way and it pops crookedly.
So no riri and no money
and no support
so again. Like Zeke.
I mean
Lila and LeeLee
Or TeeTee
HeeHEE!
Nini <3

Surgery.

You think this is good?
Nah bro.
You aint seen shit yet.
But he got the MRI at YooCeeNice
and YCN had the wizards
but not the readers
so he went to some rando
Dude who manipulated his knee
said "Yup, Ed that is a garbanzo ant
Cruciate ligament."
You mean like the harry potter encantation?
"Nah."
Ahhhh ok.
Well 7 was a page turner
so he hooped and
like on 2/22/22 or so got a new ligament
in the knee from a dead dude.
Crazy.
Left eye I mean side too.

Follow up

So the follow up appointment went down like this:
Hi.
Hi.
You good?
Yeah.
Ok.

Just kidding it was not quite like that but it basically was.

So the dude trained at The School that comes second to Cal.
1868 to forever, bitches.

Anyway back to the story sorry that was a tangent not how I planned it.

"Hi."
"knee good?"
Yeah.
Ok great.
I'm actually playing basketball again!
"Bro its like not even a month out like do PT or some shit and like slow down!"

Well……..
He was born a Ferrari. Porsche. Buggati. Silverado.
Heavey fucking duty.
Nonstop. Ed goes on feel. And the feel he goes on is his own.
San Francisco Bay Area all mf day.
NorCal. HMB.
Put those with Berkeley in ink.
Apple is the G oat. Amazon. Facebook. Google.
Do the math.
And guess what? Elon and those folks…
They have nothing on Ed.
Unfuckwittably unstoppable.
And humble too. But you
Might not know the definition of humble but here it is.

You can be confident and humble.
Be great. Let others decide if u r good.
Think about it that way.
And don't judg Ed for identifying as Harry Potter.
Even if he thinks JK got some wild ass Views from the 6 or wherever she is at.
She, like me, is imperfectly inspiring.
And just cuz you aren't
Does not mean you Can't Bey.

PAUSE.

Just chill for a second.

Take your time.

Cross the street.

Take a smoke break. Lord Knows Nick does.

Wouldn't u if you were like him?

Hum-baby

Rocky is a legend.
He knew.
Ed was QB1, pitcher….everything.
Rocky and his son and family knew
Ed had "it."
What "It" is….well only He (Rocky)
knows now. Rest in Peace,

Home body

So Rocky couldn't quite get through
Because while Ed was a Head
Of his time and wanted Head racquet
not to get knocked upside the head
from behind.
He wanted to throw down some behind.
And boy……. Well. Never mind. :)

So Ed went to NY. Went to PENN!
State.
But it was too far. For now.
So he went north.
He stated he was staying there.

And he had already abandoned
Liz and Nick who had abandoned
Him long ago.
Abandonment issues.
Welcome to the club y'all.

So he MMI IV'ed.
What's interesting is that the fake
encounters went well because although he
www.asn't an actor yet….he was a writer.
Producer. :D

Sooooooo
He aced it. Again.

Then….he was tutoring in Fairfax, VA
when the call came.

You're in.

100k per year damn near but he didn't give a fuck.

Dream wasn't deferred.
The dream was a nightmare with the light
perhaps getting dimmer still.

_____

3

In the middle, again

Sallie

Where do we start with him?
Sal lied.
How tf u ____ gonna give a dude with no
Money
No family
And just a dream
500k in student debt?
Ed had one thing: good ass credit
And yet what did Sallie say?
If Nick cosigns its a no.
If you wanna kill urself and sign up for this
Medicine shit? Aite. You on your own
Dummy.
So Sallie joined in and Sallie
May get the first black Letter.
black in this Case
Means Death. Abuse. Torture.

North of Narnia.

So Ed walks up to chronicle
The North
And it ain't Narnia, Dorothy.
It's not a bird or a plane
It's an old fucking warehouse.
I mean….I guess it goes 2 sho
fsho
That u can just make anything up and call it art.
So thats why I wrote this. Ur welcome to cumin
Read it! Front to back or back to front.
He went to that one restaurant that Jared
Went to and Not the "He went to Jared" Jared
The other one. You know which one.
Stayed at governor's mansion's inn.
Bro they deadass had some crazy human trafficking shit
Go down there, look it up. Crazy. Uptown downtown
And y'all. tryna give Oakland and Richmond
And the BROnx and Brownsville a bad name?
Nah u tripping tripping.
Ed straight outta compton damn near.
Watch out his ass gon invite u to the cookout!

Narnia and LaShawndra

Young LaShawndra………..
Aite so frfr stay wit me now
She's the first first one.
Heart of gold, pt II.
Beautiful, honest, kind, compassionate.
From SF too… duh dumbass. Y'all already no.
So LS from SF had to teeS-tuh
The rari.
Mind you at the time it was a Camry for families he was riding.
Tricked out the speakers n all but just a Toyota 4
The runner now.

Shawndra was a dime inside and out.
Well….. let's not get too graphic now this is a bedtime story for y'all. It's that put the kids to bed
Type shit.

Shawndra was the Bonnie to his Clyde in oh-five
No five-oh.
She shared her family with him.
Mind u they weren't married. No kids.
You know what it was?

Real love.

Shawndra

So while the girl was doing her thing
He was doing his
The distance was tough but they made it work
She came to him
He came.... bro chill get ya mind out the gutter.
They went up and down and all around together.
Lived the life two 20s should!
It was magical.
Hike, eat, sleep, love, talk, family, life, sex.
It was all good.
But it was young love and the compatibility
Long term was not 12......years.

Concordance City

Shawndra brought him down to stay at her mom's.
Her mom loved Ed. Who didn't?
So he worked. He cried.
He had a professionally existential crisis.
Because already he had considered death by suicide.
Twice.
Had a friend who was insanely talented gas herself like
a chamber of secrets became a Charlotte Web of lies.
Narnia.
Cancer.
And not the month errr I mean sign.
This sign was black.
Sallie. black. "Narnia" we'll call it.
Dark, dark, dark black.
Oh and how many Black students were there?
Y'all already know. Zero.
Yea fuck that place.
Shut it down.

Liz and Nick Stomping Grounds

Finally!
OMG!
Ed did it.
He got into L&N old university.
What happened there?
Crisis. Times two.
Was he pursuing the right field?
The right career?
The right woman?
Shawndra made him homeless so Ed
Dumped her.
But he wanted to make it work…
So he tried to walk back that decision.
Too late.
The first breakup.
In SF.

Ms. P.S.

She was the one
who taught him
how to play the sax
first the alto
and jazz then baritone!
the beauty of her teaching
was that she was not someone who told him that
He was too loud.
She let him rock.
Unlike Nick e liz.

The other PS

So M.S. P.S.
Was initially in the childhood lot
but Palm Springs was where
the first real
Deep
dark
bout
of depression
sunk in after FresNO!
In Fresno there was
suicide.
trauma.
shit.
cuts.
One traumatizing laceration
repair where he tried to make it
pain free but it hurt.

FresYES?

The schedule was actually reasonable
Whitney houston sang her tunes
And was a great mentor
Music.ally
butt
he was still solo dolo
AAAnd never wanted to hurt any1
so that crator created at McHospital CReamery
(MCR)
and as he held
full court PRESSedure
On the 17 year old girls
arm he didn't vomit
He didn't flinch
He felt the warm
soothing touch of her
blood as it smoothly caressed his fingertips
and the fingers on her right arm
Curled up
in a ball
as
her hand died
because she took a motorola
Actually just a RAZR
Too her right bicep and

with one slice she went through
all the brake and cephalic
Arteries.

Stanker Hospital

Trauma 1
Cancer 2
E3
For one good dude from a maad city.
Girl ueono but
He made a good
Identity for himself at this time
Geez was it something else.
Ho, so then Santa climbed down the shim Knee Rage.
and he had a crisis
Of identity
and almost apple ied
to PSYCH!!!
he applied to see em cuz that was his first choice
but ed wonder ed.
Was it love at first sight?
And if it was, was it right?
Or was it er add.
The situation where he
Simply was an adrenaline junkie?
But not a hero junkie?
Ed just was ahead of The NY Times
And wanted to do fun things
Safe! at home.

So in PS, Ed could not reach
Ms PS
and Liz and Nick were useless af.
Hunchback of notre damn.
And Zeke was struggling on his own in the
land of the supposed angels.

_____

4
In the end

Got eeem.

He landed the gig.
Ed otw to NY, C u there!
Small bitch beach town to the
land of famous coast hers.
Diversity. Complexity
Bing bang boom.
The type of gun shot wounds
You wouldn't understand.
And covid but guess what?
He did not even

blink.

Ditto mas

Right off the ocean
Brightly beached
Ed got him a spot for the first time
11
But u know wats rly weird
his neiggggghh bors
were older and v chill
but they had some multi
colored carpets on the walls
and apparently they were notorious
sooooo
when he got locked out fr what happened was this:
he knocked
they let him in
and then
he dasher and dancer and pranced right out the window
and tried to get into his
but he couldn't break through the glass
the looking glass into his own kitchen.
so he waited for the locksmith to
Undo the lock.

Michael, michael motorcycle

So Ed bought a michaelob ultra motorbike
Technically it was a mini mobile and what had happened was
some dude ripped it off him
the zak attack! one to three gone!!
and it was no more.
so ed was sad but he bought a bigger 1.
this one was a Yamaha
not to close to aha! moment
where his knees and palms got sweaty
but he didn't vomit unless he had some
corononoro viral gastro intel illness
y me da say that question passed
and he drove that shit like he stole it
but this time he was insured
thank god cuz the thing scooted like 90 on the freeway
then metoo got stolen. smdh.
Oh fOr dos.
Time for a stander upper like the nintendo Segway!
Super smashed bro.

Liz n Nick

They were holed up
Man down
Hand down
MJ
Not 23
The dubs starter pitcher.
So Liz was cracked out in the crack house
Nick was nomading up and down
from patheticA to PS
bullshiiting n shit.
running away
not on the runway
but interestingly he was
because
the runner
was funner
and the truth was in and out of the summer
Wen He
And buy he I mean Nick
was really really really
starting to fail the class
of his children
and particularly Zeke.
But who new cuz
Nick N Liz bailed.

They said their job was done.
18 and outhouse ?
Now the shit was hitting the fan…
Not just yet literally
butt soon enuf it wud.

Devil in a dress.

This woman was Satan reincarnated.
Not Judah not even Judas.
She was Black Black Flag
with the cloak and dag
Grrrrrrrr
Owl of the night.
She tricked
the corner of the club
and the lounge
Preying on men
Believe it me
she said never again
docs or atticus finch attorneys
but she did it every day
and she found the Prefect
Prey in Ed.
He wanted a partner
with no crime
But she had the good book
by her in bed when the book that she
Followed
was not the book of God
but a book by the title that many
Hos Follow.
HO TACTICS.

Its a perfect book for bitches of all genders.

———————

Date 1

What a fucking shitshow
She was loud
Obnoxious
Not feminine
Not even masculine
She was just doing one thing:
Tryna sell Ed on her nadie naughty bodie.
Rose.
She stunk to high heaven.
But he was vulnerable
and wanted a h.e.r.
so what happened was the following
She gave him a single fake kiss
And she had a fat ass.
So he texted his buddy:
She's the hottest birdie
He ever dated.
And then she got the Rona virus.
Before date 2.
It was a sign from Wuhan
that he missed.
Too bad cuz Wuhan was helping Ed
more than Rose was.
Wild.

Date2

Rose camEd in a full on ho attire.
Raincoat and brassiere in France
so he thought it was pussysmoke
pound cake at the town
with skyfall and earth wind and fire
so there were no tears in the Rain
just love in the sky
and after hours it dawned on him
that the starboy could not yet
See the madness behind the booty
cuz trust me it was a big ass booty.

_____

runner renner

lets write
she said.
lets plan our life together
lets document our love
sign a love contract
Children
marriage
Faith
Fullness
the bible was bedside
Every night
You will be my knight
in shining armor
and I
Will fade you
to
Black.

Living colors

Red is red
blue is blue
green is green
rose is red
violet is violet, violet
and white and pink makes red
Red is rage.
But she hid it under the white light
while he was straight shining bright.
So she colored his colors different
and made his green green
her yelll low was black
red was blacker
and black was black.
But dont get it box twisted
black is not complexion or color
dont braid that shit on Ed
Because as he said Rose's smell
PU when they're from you
if you are like the cocaine she blew.

Six months.

Was it financial vulnerability?
Was it generational trauma?
Was it Ms. colored colors?
Was it Ab use?
Was it the job Ed had?
Who knows?
But six months in.
They moved in.
Too get her.
Shit.

———

2415

7 floors.
He got to the top.
She said don't stop.
He said make a friend
She found the daughter of a noctor
And flocked her with
a Proctor protocol
and they lived happily ever after.
NOT.
Well at the time they were pretty happy tbh.
She worked. He worked.
They ate.
She vibrated.
And Rose RosEd her next vino
from Italy
Where her fam bam bombed from the land de la Mami.
Y
Ahora yo pienso
que ella pretended to hablar
Espanol
 so she could fake it her whole
Entire Life.
And brainwash him just like Her Good Book.
Hoe with some 8008s and a fake ass @$$.

All equal

Ed worked
She twerked
And in the intense unit where the
Ward revealed just as much psychiatric illness as medical illness
He wanted all equal
All fair
No favors
No special treatment
Even if they looked like him
Even if they acted like her
He gave the plastics repair to a murderer
He treated the homeless drunk
The same his female counterpart who
Just wanted Motrin but not ibuprofen
Or was it ibuprofen and not Motrin?
Allergies make you AHHH Choo Choo
He wanted the rich treated the same as the poor
Because wealth has no correlation to rich spirit
And covid wreaked havoc on everyone from young adults to old ones
But interest ing Lee
It kept the kids safe.
Me pienso que this was by duh-sign.

JFK heart attack

From Vegas to Houston to atlanta to Nueva York
Doc was there for everyone
He helped all patients from all stripes
All levels of all learners
And then one day
.....
.....
Boom.
He dropped dead.
The House of God took another one
Who forgot to put the oxygen gas mask on
Himself.
First.
He needed care too.
Left behind a beautiful family and a community
That would never forget
Doc was the legend of that spot.
If there is a piece of peace up there, he is running it.
Selfless to the city that never sleeps.

Techs and cleaners

EVS and transport
And clerks
And RuNners
I mean you know whats cray cray?
Ed
Got all Ong
Well with all of them ex Sept.
A lot of the ego crazed cowerkers
They were werking and for sum
Razon
They ignored the people that Horton
Heard
Because a person is a people
No matter
Their
In come.

Red head

U see
It was the worst kept secret that
They liked each other
And she was super glued to him
At trabajo
And she said maybe dos anos
Ella would even Ven ture
Sure con el
Pero
The kraman had an amor
Color of her love was black
Now imma bust ya chops hardcore
If y'all think the color of love is
Ever
Ever
Eve
Rrrrrrrr
Lo mismo as the color of one's soul
Bc colorism is absolutely fucking bullshit.
Butt
(And not the good, big, juicy kind)
So.
He really tried to limit sending signs
Outside of work ones cuz she modeled
Fashion and she is ….. well red can mean

Love.
Even if her complexion was light and
Complexion has zero correlation or causation to the color
Of her soul.
Or his for that Mat ter.
But maybe what Ed tHOt was his type
Was not his ty pe after all?
Send his ass back to the motherland.
Ireland.
Dublin.
....
He gotta go there frfr. T'ell him!

Zeke

He was in n out
Not of burgers
But of consciousness
Not because of Ness
I mean the one in smash
Super smash bros
But because the issue was he could not find himself
Pills
Weed
Sober
Drunk
The thing is this.
Boom Hers and Hims and Theys and Thems
Pros or nouns or adject eves It
don't matter
As Drake and MJ said.
Because a lost soul is a lost soul.
And it all started at la casa de la familia
Donde Donda was Liz; and Nick
Was just an absent father.
You see.
His complexion was fair
But his soul was lost
Not black but lost in the abyss.

BUT that is no excuse!
He is was will be a turible father, Chuck.
If ur straight its possible dat
Dat adult HOOD
Is avoided if and only if
The father steps up.
If not at least shit let a step father step in
Cuz he just a fat her no off hence.
Zeke was spiraling alone.

Final

Lights…class…action!
Ed at the top of the board
Running the code
Blues and reds
While they were running code
Browns
in the back
cuz like em ed
was evictem of a violent
spiritual crime
The diagnosis?
Munchausen.
And munchausen
By proxy.
Ed had a feeling.
Zeke was so deep in the sunken place
he had a 1 over 0 chance
of Get TingTing Out.

The theory

Borderline personality disorder
is the most underdiagnosed condition
in the USA if not the world
Emotional instability
Hard to
Judge
the execution of emotions
but the lability
Not stability
of the fragility
Of Liz and Zeke
Rubbed off on Ed et al
and what happened was
BPD and BiPolar ex Disorder
colloquially have overlap
cuz Nick's dumb ass thinks hes a fucking
doctor
That bitch ass ho.
Men can be hoes too y'all….
anyway
The
Anorexia combined with the depression
with the
PSYCH
hosis

with the manipulation
and it was a straight clusterfuck
No gay needed.
But here's The Secret:
BPD is likely due to MHS imho.
There's a DSM VI starter for ya
Supposed specialists. Smdh.

_____

About the Author

Elijah Abramson, M.D. is an artist and scientist who is also a board-certified American physician specializing in all emergencies, currently practicing in the state of California. His wide-ranging personal and professional life experiences continue to expand his knowledge base as well as desire to share it. He has lived and worked in (as well as travelled to) a variety of resourced and under-resourced communities. He hopes to share his art through multiple mediums to bring light where there is or was darkness. He lives in Sacramento, CA.

Made in the USA
Middletown, DE
18 June 2025

77047998R10066